GOD'S SPIDER

ALSO BY CYRIL DABYDEEN

Fiction

The Wizard Swami (Peepal Tree, 1989)
Dark Swirl (Peepal Tree, 1989; rptd. 2007)
Jogging in Havana (Mosaic Press, 1992)
Sometimes Hard (Longman, 1994). Young adult.
Berbice Crossing (Peepal Tree, 1996)
Black Jesus and Other Stories (TSAR Publications, 1997).
My Brahmin Days and Other Stories (TSAR Publications, 2000)
North of the Equator (Beach Holme, 2001)
Drums of My Flesh (TSAR Publications, 2005)
Play A Song Somebody: New and Selected Stories (Mosaic Press, 2005)
Short Stories of Cyril Dabydeen (Guyana Classics, 2011).

Poetry

Poems in Recession (Guyana, 1972)
Goatsong (Mosaic, 1977)
Distances (Fiddlehead, 1977)
This Planet Earth (Borealis, 1979)
Heart's Frame (Vesta Publications, 1979)
Elephants Make Good Stepladders (Third Eye,1982)
Islands Lovelier Than a Vision (Peepal Tree,1986)
Coastland: New and Selected Poems (Mosaic, 1989)
Stoning the Wind (TSAR, Toronto, 1994)
Born in Amazonia (Mosaic, 1995)
Discussing Columbus (Peepal Tree, 1997)
Imaginary Origins: New and Selected Poems (Peepal Tree, 2004)
Uncharted Heart (Borealis Press, 2008)
Unanimous Night (Black Moss Press, 2009)

CYRIL DABYDEEN

GOD'S SPIDER

PEEPAL TREE

First published in Great Britain in 2014
Peepal Tree Press Ltd
17 King's Avenue
Leeds LS6 1QS
UK

ISBN 13: 9781845232443

Supported using public funding by
ARTS COUNCIL
ENGLAND

ACKNOWLEDGEMENTS

Thanks to the editors of the following in which some of these poems appeared in an original form: *Prairie Schooner* (USA), The *Warwick Review* (UK), *Icfar University Journal of Commonwealth Literature* (India), *Rampike* (University of Windsor, Canada), *The Arts Journal* (Guyana/ Caribbean), *South Asian Ensemble* (Canada), and *Canadian Literature* (University of British Columbia, Canada).

"Dead White Men" appeared in *Canadian Studies Today: Responses from the Asia-Pacific*, eds. Stewart Gill and R.K. Dhawan (Prestige Books, India); and "Tryst with Destiny" appeared in *Various Cultures, Various Readings*, ed. B. Hariharan, et al. (Creative Books, India).

"Wilson Harris: Land Surveyor" appeared in *Another Life*, eds. Melanie Joseph-Vilain and Judith Misrahi-Barak. Collaboration: EMMA (Etudes Montpellieraines du Monde Anglophone) at Universite Paul-Valery Montpellier, and "Centre Interlangues TIL" (Texte, Image, Langage) at Universite de Bourgogne, France.

I also thank the Ontario Arts Council for their support. And to Jeremy Poynting and Hannah Bannister (Peepal Tree Press) I express a special gratitude.

In the middle of the road
I found myself in a dark wood.

Dante, *Divine Comedy*

CONTENTS

FOUR

ONE

ABSOLUTE INTERIORITY

— after Carlos Fuentes

The South Americans
and the Greeks have it — and
some Americans, too: knowing
about the poem's inner life,
or whether you're barking
up the wrong tree.

Now, Charybdis, what
I've bolstered, and keep
thinking long about —
the poem's kernel — where it
wants to be most of all

as I keep making promises,
now with Homer and Odysseus
in distant seas after another storm,
somewhere near Ithaca, or next in
the Himalayas with Alexander the Great,

mountains appearing from
the clouds with a current of their
own, in a different territory
with the rains coming
down hard — all now being
part of the poem's inner life,

so I keep wanting it to be
no other way than with the Greeks
or with the Mexicans,
staring up at the face
of Quetzalcoatl eating
someone's heart out,

or with Walt Whitman who knew best
about a chrysalis on a lilac tree,
or a pupa becoming a caterpillar,
the butterfly spreading out
its wings and flying away...

HOW I FATHOM MYSELF

It's how I fathom myself
breaking down barriers
with an understanding

of who I am not.
Oh, not that again,
I hear you say.

What I yearn for
are open spaces, being
everywhere now,

discovering myself
anew, my heart
throbbing

in the desire to be
only with you,
my lungs, nostrils

heaving with fire,
odd circumstances,
or dreams again –

what I've encountered
from long ago –
telling you once more

with curses, wounds –
fervour only – who I really am,
telling you, no other.

IF WE MUST TALK

If we must talk let there
be words, not this silence,
the mouth's corkscrew
shape again;

a voice travelling far
to where it wants to be,
like ripples in an ocean,
the wind's consonants

hissing as never before
in wider seas,
the mind's own place –
nowhere else –

what I've conceived
long ago – my senses
haywire, and being
somewhere else –

in one territory –
what I keep imagining
without a warning, now
being a wayfarer of sorts.

FATHER POEM

My father, lost for forty days
and forty nights, he told
us, in the Amazon
with tribes unknown,

newly discovered,
in territories never seen before,
shooting up at an airplane
high above like a hoax.

All this, I kept thinking,
my father might have
imagined, or just yarned about –
being too long in the hot sun –

worlds bigger than himself
with new instincts,
as I too look up at the clouds –
at what keeps appearing,
       nowhere else.

ANNALS OF TIME

— Northrop Frye in Guyana, 1980

A place to go to, or come from —
now to shore up a country,
or a government, though politicians
have their own way with autocracy,
or sheer mimicry. Or it's to be
again with Sir Walter Raleigh
in the Orinoco seeking El Dorado
as the harpy eagle soars above the tree canopy,
or where the anaconda moves
quietly below, and the jaguar
sniffs at raindrops in the middle ground,
a boundary, from long ago — annals
of lost time. I keep looking up at thunder
and lightning, a storm breaking loose
because of government paralysis;
or facing up again to what's
our common ancestry, as Jung
would have it — mere racial pride —
as we keep being who we are
                    — in fearful symmetry.

CANECUTTER'S MANDOLIN

Here in this village –
     not Venice
in the Mediterranean –
     where he plays
the mandolin after another
     long day in the cane fields

Villagers listen to him,
     while his wife's lips
are set tight, wondering
     who he might have
been as he keeps on
     strumming

Imagining him as
     a classical guitarist,
Flamenco style, but hearing
     now a villager's pain,
as he holds the mandolin
     closer to his chest

Then everyone applauds,
     a sound not unlike
tropical rain, but his wife
     thinks he's only
sotted with rum –
     nothing more

Later he'll pick
     a fight with her,
plucking the guitar strings
     harder, chopping
cane-sounds in his ears
     all the while

LAUGHING LEPERS

— after George Barker

1.
Coming out of shadows, caves, catacombs,
they look back at me and make faces,
turn round and wave. Sages of old. One hand
lifts, inviting me to enter. Let Ben Hur acknowledge
a mother and sister from bygone days in a movie-world.

2.
Paul Gauguin keeps painting knobbly faces,
women of Tahiti, with distinct shapes and forms –
a determined style. See, my own artist's hand's
at it; I am also coming out of a cave,
with shadows all around.

3.
Devil's Island, Papillon flutters, wings beating:
how do I escape this hellhole of a prison?
It's all I ever want, you know, to be with you
always when it's dark – the doldrums
I can never escape from in Cayenne.

4.
Other places – Iraq, Afghanistan – beckon
because of what runs deep in my veins,
under the integument of skin. Abu Ghraib,
you say?It's what I won't accept, and will
reject at a glance, a turnaround.

5.
Bihar or Mumbai – places where I don't want to be –
the stump of a hand protruding from a shirtsleeve,
being in the village where I was born, the man living
on familiar Third Street I look at,
hands before my face, and balk.

6.
I take up the paint brush, a camera or a pen,
and I laugh because of what remains unseen,
what yet beckons – what Plato or Bacon also
contemplated at odd moments. Do I see
another distant place where the horizon bends?

7.
In the media's glare, as the paparazzi take mug shots –
one lunges forward. Look out! – fashion magazines pin
their hopes on everyone flaunting sex appeal. On Fifth
Avenue, Manhattan, I swagger along, John Travolta-style.
Do I take another deliberate step in a movie scene?

8.
I wave a flag; it's freedom I am after! Surviving,
where we're not supposed to be, yet being with
Gauguin, Ben Hur, Papillon looking from secret corners,
alleyways, eyes staring out from dark sockets;
I heave in, harder, if you know my will!

9.
Cup at my lips, wafer on my tongue, the choir
singing. In church, temple, mosque, synagogue –
all where I seek solace – what you offer me;
what I know because of you, being my true self,
believe me, as nothing is what it seems!

FOREIGN TERRITORY

1

What I want you to know,
being here with you,
the body's shape's
a foreign territory,
with signposts

To be loyal to, though it's
the urge to be with Odysseus
again, crossing the sea
to Ithaca, the sun now on
a wilderness of sorts

The horizon mirroring
longing and desire,
as I come to you with
the body's need
of another country

Thick forest with
hair falling down
like strands of wire.
But do I want
to be a foreigner

Where bramble bush
only will proliferate,
and not be somewhere else
with blood, synapses,
love of a special kind?

2

In thrall again, meeting
you with passport in hand,
crouched on bended
knees, unheralded

What I will let you know
about over time – moon-face
concave or convex,
orange-red as night comes

the sun now dying with
flamenco ease, longer
days and nights ahead –
what I accuse you of

Imperialist, you!

THE BORDER

No human being is illegal.   —— Elie Wiesel

It's not where I wanted to be,
adrift, facing barbed-wire fences,
palings, tunnels and border guards,
yet being here with you makes more
than a disturbance of the spirit.

Anonymous in my new skin,
false clothes, glancing over
my shoulder and moving
sideways, always in a hurry,
I look over the horizon,
to the curve and bend of it,
and dream of burnt brick roadways
crossing the map of an old country.

Oh, what did I look forward to,
saying it again and again,
but being in another place
in another time – paradise
in someone else's backyard,
or Joni Mitchell's parking lot –
under a cochineal sun
and palm trees that I keep
telling you about, not where
it's cold as I grit my teeth,
inhaling hard in the solid air,
but where, with nowhere else
to go, breathing in the new scent,
I raise a flag, finally.

COLD IN CANADA

for Philip Niland

Shit, it's cold, he says, but
I say, in England you don't
know what cold really is.
Come to Canada

where you will feel
your teeth chattering,
chill winds a-blowing
and feel your bones rattle;

come to Winnipeg, prairie heartland,
or somewhere like it,
where West Indian immigrants
cower, never to recover;

where you will contemplate
living like an Inuit in an igloo,
hunkered down with blankets,
wrapped in whale blubber,

pretending to be a polar bear,
woollen all over. Or you might try
yoga, with oms and chanting
mantras to keep warm;

or revert to swallowing rum,
though that's not so spiritual.
Shit, it's cold, with more wind
blowing – chinook or coulees –

so you can pretend you're in the Arctic
for real, going on the Franklin expedition,
searching for the Northwest Passage,
trapped in the ice.

Shit, it's cold, you say,
though you're now there
to stay, indeed being far
from the tropics.

MOVING ON

It's more than the senses,
the body's weight,
but words, syntax,

a vocabulary most of all,
an almanac of sorts
to come to grips with,

determined to be close
to you in my style;
to let it be known

what I think about
in odd circumstances,
a journey I begin

again with you –
time's hourglass;
what I will

reminisce about,
or never want to hear
about again, separating

myself from you –
where I never wanted
to be in the first place –

unexpected movements
really, the body reshaping
itself because of too dear

offspring – what I care about
in the momentum
of blood and bone;

holding my hands
above my head with
the encyclopedia

of the years –
telling you this
once more.

PART TWO

ANTS
(after Margaret Atwood)

Making ants interesting,
putting words together is
the human itch or stain,
as the insects crawl about
being busier bodies than
the rest of us manage – indeed,
a singular prompt to keep building
as the leaf-cutter ant carries
more than twice its body-weight
on its back. True workhorses –
George Orwell, beware!

They teach us a real work-ethic
and other social values,
wending their antlered way,
or looking like a rhinoceros; and
nothing will stop them, not even
an anteater bent on causing
disturbance by scratching hard
on the ground. Now being who
we are, we move around with our
festering geopolitics, leave ants
less and less terrain, though knowing
there are more ants around than all
other species – socialists all!

But ants keep being ants on their mounds
or grassy knolls close by a river;
and some ants will swim like
a fish or fly like a bird, though
a lone ant will pause before
a caterpillar clinging elephant-like
to a leaf, blocking its path. Indeed

ants will prevail, I say to students
in my creative-writing class,
or as Atwood would have it,
what prevails is the desire
to make ants as interesting
as possible, without angst
or Antwood, but only with
a writer's lasting itch.

GOD'S SPIDER

i

The place where he kept being,
or dreamed about, the firmament of
celestial stars above the tree canopy
in the hinterland, his instinct
with the ways of Carib, Arawak,
Waspishana, forebears infused
with auguries from the ancient Greeks,
and journeys in the making –
always the mind or spirit's own.

Spinning a web, he glanced back
into the memory of each tree,
the fallen leaves like a vestige
of tapestry, as the jaguar sniffs
at the river's mouth, then ahead
to the strain of portage up
the rapids, and threat of tacoubas
hidden in the river's chocolate mirk,
things he must come to grips with
in his dreamer's maze.

ii

Still spinning, he looks up
as the transcendent cliff-face
looms higher, its waterfalls, rapids,
started long ago from origins
in the Amazon, ready to explore
new space or territory,
celestial always.

Then the passage through neural tunnels,
caves, labyrinthine, Borges-like,
everything spun, rounded out,
seeking what's hidden in shadow,
voyaging with the one named Donne,
the boat steering a new course
in Cuyuni waters, or arriving
at the Mission with the
reverent Catholic Fathers.

What the Caribs contrived
with bone-flute, memory-tunes,
he wrote about in another
entry in his journal: charting
the known or unknown
sources in the hinterland,
moving closer in time's
solitude, or resonance, with
a long drawn-out silence.

REVISITED

Slender brown fingers release
bright balloons high
into the dark sea
                    Jean Szeles

i

The place I've come from,
meeting you at the zenith
beyond the sea or ocean,

an emerald forest with
branches hanging low,
liana spreading amongst

what I may have forgotten
to tell you about,
crossings on my mind,

words carved, images
I recall again and again,
because like Raleigh

in the Orinoco,
I'm a dreamer with maps –
and now what else

do I imagine…
being in the Tower,
Elizabethan always?

ii

Looking upwards,
a balloon rising
in the air,

coconuts appear
pneumatic in the sun,
emblems keeping us

together once more
with more longings,
desires, the kernel

of a dream coming true,
that I will wrestle with:
build the poem's own artefact,

brick by brick, or an
altar in hallowed time,
new rhythms in the air,

or a darker sea.

DEAD WHITE MEN

History's about dead white men,
      he tells me, in more than jest,
about Barack Obama's winning ways;
      and his son's now studying
at the University of Chicago
      in changing times,
changing ways.

Another tells of his wife, a junior
      school teacher, being given
a five-day suspension because
      she'd gone home to a school
reunion in her native New Zealand,
      where she hoped to meet
Maoris "from way back" –

words said to the Ottawa School Board
      officials who frowned,
thinking only of punitive measures
      for her having skipped classes;
I mull over the Royal Reader
      of my junior school days
in British Guiana, and Queen Elizabeth's
      coronation –

the mug I'd been given,
      a memento still with me
in Canada, my own treasured
      gift of lost-and-found.

THE OLD MAN

In the terrain/what terrain/that
place where we never want to be
but will be in nevertheless/

in Kenya/or some place else
with origins at the fingertips/
what continues to mould us

as offspring/ tremors now deep
in the veins/vocal chords/
memory/ binding us together

as a Luo /or a Kiyuyu/
a remembered place/hinterland
or savannah/bringing us together

Livingstone/Burton/Rhodes/
the voice's rasp/Jefferson/
Lincoln/who else in former days?

Being in the Indian Ocean/ or is it
America where we don't feel
we belong/but where we want to be?

Hawaii/Indonesia/bones we carry/
what Leakey or some other might
have understood/who first lived here

the Old Man's vocal chords/an
ancient song/what's self-evident
we've carried in us/from the start

BICENTENARY

(Slave trade, 2007)

— for Rachel Manley

i
Who says there are no ghosts
here, no tremors of the heart,
windows rattling,
doors shaking from long ago,
oceans coming closer...

ii
Who's pleading?
What voices from
the dead, or undead,
from what plantation's shores,
in silent moments,
cries from the heart?

iii
I look far out,
high up from the mast,
imagining what's real,
being only above deck...
yet going under... what the
stars never foretell.

TOMBSTONE (TOBAGO)

She was a mother without knowing it, and a wife without letting
her husband know it except by her kind indulgences to him.
      — Betty Stivens (1783): died in childbirth; maybe a slave.

Mesmerized by what's old
      or new, I imagine who
you might have been long ago —
      Betty Stivens, woman
with wiles, desires of your own —
      forbearance too; what you
kept intact for years on these shores,
      come from another place,
washed up like coral. Who
      knows what adventures, what
by a man or husband you endured,
      though I know you suffered long
a mother's pain. Memory-veins beating,
      we keep looking at the tombstone,
almost too personal here in lava-shaped
      Tobago, this island coral formed
after the volcano came up long ago.

(June 5, 2011)

38

PIGGOT-MAN

— after C.L.R. James

He would swing and sway
behind the stumps,
keeper that he was,
and whoever could bowl
fast, like Miller or Lindwall,
Piggie kept at it,
stretching out, then leaping
forward, being right there
behind the wicket, ready
to stump you out –
the bails down as you
lurched forward. What Piggy
knew best was standing straight up,
then crouching again. Ah,
many said he could have been
the best damned wicketkeeper
around, but they wouldn't
select him for London or Kingston,
not for a Test Match because
he ain't white – this all in colonial times.
What Piggie knew in his heart,
and I say: he was the best –
in Trinidad or anywhere else,
moving far
         – beyond a boundary.

COMMONWEALTH

"What do they know of cricket who only cricket know."

My New Zealand-born friend
gives me for Christmas
C.L.R. James' *Beyond a Boundary*
in the change-room at the pool.

We talk about cricket
and the West Indies' glory days,
the Commonwealth again,
though he's keener on rugby,

the All Blacks, the Maoris
making their warlike cries;
but he'd also played cricket,
being a spin bowler. He tells

me too how he took part in
a New York marathon (he'd lived
in the US, studied in Arkansas
and California).

Now I regale him with our connections,
about how I'd once drilled
a group of scholars at a conference
here in Ottawa about how much

they really knew about
the Commonwealth, and how they
looked at me agape when
I asked: "Who's Richie Benaud?"

Yes, one woman did burst out:
"A cricketer!"
– but she was
from Australia.

For Graham and me –
going beyond a boundary
in wintry Ottawa, not far from
the Governor General's residence

where W.G. Grace once played,
English always, and I would read
Tunapuna-born James and score sixes
in my mind (as Benaud would say),

nothing else being in the air,
thinking of where we've come
from in our now longer –
Commonwealth days.

–Dec. 18, 2012

THE GLASS-BOTTOMED BOAT

What's on the other side,
the underbelly, meeting you
in a rendezvous of sorts, like
being wayward again because
of the body's urge, the senses' need;
and what it will tell you about
is the story's beginning, not ending.

It's where to contemplate
a new source of narrative that
Freud might have understood, or
Einstein foretold: a wild craving
or burning, with fantasy being
in the mix. A place to think…
more carefully, but how carefully?

Peering down at thickets of arteries,
lymph nodes that keep being
knotted in, and arms and legs
splayed out, thighs gripping harder,
much harder, being somewhere
in the marine forest, or under-sea hills,
the ground-earth being everywhere.

Now meeting you again at the glass,
with grunts and groans,
an irreverent sigh – your forehead
arched, eyelids peeled back –
longings, then disdain because
of unrequited love – what the text
foreshadows – narrative ongoing.

It keeps going round and round in my head,
      making me dizzy – as one jury
member expresses humility and blushes,
      while for another it's all about ego,
sheer ego, in deciding what's the best book.
      Ah, the winner, the critic nods,
acknowledging some new writing trend –
      artistic finesse with suspense;
or it's about the character-development
      found in one book; how such-and-such a writer
is distinctive in voice – a wizard with words.
      But another jury member disdains making
such judgements, her sensitivity being…
      to sisterhood – not unlike in a college
sorority. Then comes the charge of an
      old boys' club. So what else matters,
but ideology, cultural identity mixed in
      with gender analysis, or, is it psychological
analysis with cultivated angst? And who's
      writing with an agenda in mind, or
malice aforethought? Or passion for words only?
      Indeed now it's a new school of
literary criticism with the likes of Terry Eagleton;
      so what's the deal with the intended
being with the old school of Leavis, Richards,
      Brooks, and who else, has been upended,
with Derrida and Foucault much in vogue
      in America? Wimsatt and Beardsley out, too,
for Fish? Stale metaphors compounded.
Never mind rhetoric or logic, it's the jury member's
      prerogative to decide what's the best book,
even being at a loss for words. Indeed inspiration comes
      in more ways than one, as more books are
printed, and authors keep doing the rounds –

each new work being what readers
must always contend with. So beware of
        the juror who refuses to give in to emotion,
insisting on nothing being subjectified – no decision
        made nor consensus reached, but what
will last longest, despite deconstruction,
        or post-modernism, or what's not downright
meta-fictional, as if the reader no longer exists.
        Ah, now I am adrift, Crusoe-like,
floating to an uninhabited island, where
        I will find refuge in the first or last book
published, a lifetime of reading yet to come.

        But I will insist upon what can be called a classic,
not what's dead-ended, or locked in one place –
        as I make my own choice, finally.

ARISTOTLE SAID

the brain's an organ
      for cooling the blood –
such nice manners,
      I hear you say,

being kind to give tranquillity
      to heart and lungs
when meeting others, especially
      those with vile tempers

(but never your own, you think),
      cooling what comes
from the spleen or viscera –
      the body in motion.

There's pure water in the brain
      that comes from a mountain,
which puts the lava of the volcanic
      heart at rest –

what the Ancients
      thought they knew best,
but I have a different story to tell –
      trying to imagine you.

PART THREE

AFTER THE DEITIES

I
The deities came to me
at will – believe me,
I had no choice,

wanting to be myself
with ancestry only
at the crossroads

where I was born,
being adrift
in a new country,

in the Orinoco,
voices beckoning.
Now, indentured,

I tried to resist it
with small talk of
Calcutta, grimacing

because of the "dark waters" –
in English only –
waves rising higher

in a storm, and sails
flapping hard,
the ship battered,

a nightmare that
I couldn't escape
even below deck

or high up in the masthead,
asking the stars for
an auspicious moment

because India's deities
are all around, and what's
ordained I will

have to contend with.
Or is it another monsoon,
rain coming down hard

on ashes scattered
after a funeral pyre?
I will let you know.

II

Mirage in the hot sun
in a desert in Rajasthan,
or Uttar Pradesh –

the deities pulling
at my eyelids because
I'm near the equator.

Hoodwinked by time,
the tides rising
much higher,

a plantation life
I will reckon with,
being reborn, I believe,

with new instincts,
reincarnation –
more or less!

The god Shiva now
jeering at me,
I'd fasted long,

being an ascetic
of sorts, having
the sheer nerve for it –

a spiritual finesse.
I'll keep at it
in the new place;

I'll let you know –
will-power only,
my senses alert.

III

Conquest relived,
or what I've never
understood before,

nor believed in –
self-anointed as I may be,
appearing divine,

confronting more gods;
indeed, what will last longest
in changing times.

SHAKIRA MEETS SHIVA:
SWEET DREAMS

Here be monsters
lurking deep within,
whose demons keep

entreating us more than
the Ancients ever did;
longing or desire

compelling us to be
who we're not,
memory dogging us

more than the Neanderthal
senses will allow, the mind
going to another place

or another time with the likes
of Shakira, as more doubts
come to the fore when Shiva appears,

and I'm wanting to be
with Atman only,
looking up at the stars,

outshining all else,
amidst more heavenly
bodies, as hips sway

on the diurnal stage,
Shiva making a face
after a lingering look

at his consort, Parvati.
Disclaiming selves
because of who we think

we're not, what I want
to tell you most of all,
about true love —

eager to be someone else —
being transcendent only,
eternal in timelessness.

Birth and rebirth
        considered
at the time of
        the Golden Egg,
as the Brahman
        figured where life
literally began,

where all humans
        come from before
birth in the Cosmos'
        own shape –
what the swami
        first imagined
before Plato's
        allegory of the caves;

Maya, or life's
        timelessness,
I contemplate –
        falsifying
everything because
        of words
superimposed
        from deep within,

not unlike Coleridge's
        theory of aesthetics,
in his *Biographia Literaria*,
        which the swami
never thought of –
        closing his eyes,
humming a mantra
        signifying nothing.

SAROJINI NAIDU: LETTER
TO DAUGHTER LEILAMANI

"I can never forget your eyes – you are the Indian poet."
— Countess Tolstoy

My beloved little child,
this is my last night in Europe,
in this great foreign, arrogant continent
where through my song and speech
and struggle I have won a place for India.

Now I am glad to set my face
homewards once more to serve our country
with speech and song and struggle,
but the one poignant regret I have
is that I left you behind – alone,

you, with your brave, beautiful, rebellious
ignorant youth; you, with your
passionate, implacable temperament, so
audaciously sure of itself, its aims, its
innocence, its lofty ideals and lively desires

and dreams, and yet so threatened
with perils and pitfalls, all the more
to be feared because you are so fearless,
so impatient of tender counsel
born of bitter experience…

My little girl, how I have tried
to shield and guard you, to save you
from the suffering and disillusion
arising from your own too eager,
too exacting demands
upon friendships and affections,

unused and unable to endure
the strain of such insistent demands...

When you have resented what you thought
was an attempt to curb and hamper you,
I assure you, my darling, there was
nothing but the purest, deepest
comprehending mother-love, trying
to safeguard you from your own
impetuous nature and impulses –
so harshly misjudged and misconstrued
by even those who seemed to you
most likely to understand and appreciate...

It is because I wanted to protect you
from suffering such as I had to endure
in my youth, because my temperament
and ideas were different – they are different
from what the world accepts and
understands – that I tried to guide you...
But as the French poet said,
"A chacun son infini" – and you
must find and realise your own soul
in the infinity of its own loneliness, my child.

Only remember that you are an Indian girl,
and that puts upon you a heavier burden
than if you were an English girl, born
to a heritage of freedom. Remember that
you have to help India to be free
and the children of tomorrow to be
freeborn citizens of a free land.
Therefore, if you are true to your
country's need, you must recognise
the responsibility of your Indian womanhood.

Nothing in your speech or action
should cause the progress of Indian
women to suffer, nothing in yourself
should give room for wretched reactionary
slave-minds to say, "This comes of giving
too much education and freedom to our women."
Think over it, my darling. You are not free
in the sense of being a law unto yourself,
in defiance of all existing tradition in our
country, for freedom is the heaviest
bondage since it entails duties,
responsibilities and opportunities
from which slaves are immune...

Noblesse oblige! and the ampler the liberty,
the narrower the right to do as one pleases;
and you, my friend of delight, you must shine
as a foremost gem in the crown of India's freedom...
You have in you all the seeds of true greatness:
so be great, my little child, fulfil yourself nobly
in accordance with all the profound and beautiful
impulses and ideals of your nature... but always
remembering that you are the symbol of India.
And may God prosper you in all things.

I love you, my baby, you will never know how dearly,
and with what anxious and yearning tenderness...
Well, goodnight my little Papi, and good bye!
You are the guardian of my Jewel of Delight...
Beware! Be faithful to your trust and keep
the treasure of your soul incorruptible.
                    — Marseille, France (4 March 1921)

("Sarojini Naidu: *Selected Letters 1890s to 1940s*,"
ed. Makarand Paranjape, *Kali for Women*, 1996.)

HOLY MEN
—B.C. 326

The naked holy men
sat for hours in the sun
concentrating on the Godhead —
the Universe as One.

Alexander the Great
who conquered
the known world
was dumbfounded
watching the holy men

here in the Indus Plain
in the sun. He kept
wondering what
strange wisdom
they might impart.

So he asked his bright
young officer, Onesicritus,
to go and speak to the holy men,
find out what they knew.

The holy men told Onesicritus,
through his interpreters,
the only knowledge
they had to pass on

would be like trying
to make water flow
through layers
of mud…

Aaahh…

TSUNAMI

1

The sea is not the sea any more, but
a body being boisterous – waves
coming in at a moment's notice;

this is what I've willed myself to believe,
as this man tells me about being
above ground in Galle or Matara

in Sri Lanka – now a Tamil's
curse, as the hills will
no longer rise up, he says.

2

In Aceh province in Indonesia, or
Thailand's Phuket island, where
the Indian Ocean's Buddhist

monks meditate longest,
praying with a conch's noise,
or a voice's echo, that comes

from a mosque below,
the minaret falling lower
as more waves come full force,

all being swept away
like a rag doll. From
afar I imagine everyone

running, the clamour for safety,
or yearning for forgiveness
because of the sea's wrath,

as elephants bound off to
higher ground, then start
moving in a circle. This

man tells me about fate
according to Buddha,
a reminder of what's below

the sea floor, tectonic plates
shifting, an earthquake,
a Richter scale's reckoning –

what this man really fears and
anthems, canticles. I heave in
hard and breathe out longest.

3
Hearts beating faster, who
will swear like a villager
with a cast-net, drawing in

his breath, as I hear from afar,
monks all around, with aquamarine
waters deep down; and no one

will really know about
the true currents, or what
the Buddha's lofty aims are.

I think about an avatar, too,
contemplating the elephants'
noiseless path, tramping along

as waves wash everything away,
what I want to I say to you…
about what will remain.
                    (Dec. 22, 2009)

BUDDHA IN OTTAWA

The moment he turns around,
holiness in his veins,
I see his face's expression

as he closes his eyes, and those
passing by look at him askance
here in the park, and try to avert

their eyes, not wanting to catch
him red-handed with his eyelids
peeled back, exophthalamus.

He smiles from a far place within,
humming oms, an echo-chamber
from the Ganges – Rishikesh,

with saints and sadhus at Bodh Gaya.
Now by the Rideau River, under the maple tree
here in Ottawa, thinking it's the bodhi only

in this man's face, or voice, I will
remember, closing my own eyes,
faith or belief truly expressed.

QUALIFIED MONKEY-CATCHER

A riff

The Municipal Corporation of Delhi
is no longer preoccupied
with civic services: garbage collection,
road repair and the like. Now it's under
a court order to catch monkeys
that run amok through the city,
to relocate them to a wildlife sanctuary

at the edge of town. But the MCD
says it can't hire monkey-catchers
despite running dozens of newspaper ads,
scouring or scanning the monkey-management
world. Indeed only one monkey catcher
turned up to undertake this work.

This resulted in difficulties in dealing with
the monkey menace. Reliance on untrained labour
meant the monkeys were winning, the city said.
"This is no joking matter!" The deputy mayor of Delhi,
S.S. Bajwa, died of head injuries – the poor
man had fallen from his terrace after being
set upon by a troop of monkeys while
reading his morning paper.

See, monkeys are trapped, but not killed
because of reverence for Hanuman,
the Hindu monkey god, and because
a powerful animal-rights lobby insists
monkeys be humanely relocated. Since 2007,
the MCD says, it has relocated some 12,850 monkeys.
But thousands more continue to leap
in packs from rooftop to rooftop.

They have also shown a preference
for colonizing the area of New Delhi,
home to many government offices.
Now some ministries have full-time
employees patrolling the outside of the buildings,
catapulting pebbles at macaques who reach into
open windows for snacks or, failing that,
for computer keyboards, handbags and files.

Ah, last year, senior officials of the state
electoral commission complained to the MCD
that monkeys repeatedly trashed their offices,
chewed through their computer cables, rendering
them unable to work. Now the MCD wants
monkey responsibilities shifted to the wildlife
branch of the Delhi state government. What else?

But it has only three monkey-catchers on its roster,
and upping the price paid per monkey
from $8 to $15 over the past four years has made
no difference. City spokesman, Deep Matheu,
explained that religious sentiment keeps
some people away from the job; but the main problem
is people are scared of monkeys – not gods.

TRYST WITH DESTINY

No place to go,
no place to find a destiny

palpable or unreal
but being who I am,

here in India
at the midnight hour,

the moon's phase
an auspicious moment,

Nehru's most of all.
With astrology at my fingertips,

and a dot mark on my forehead,
(a bindi, I will fully accept,

such as worn by the likes of
Julia Roberts – women being

who they are with identifying
marks), I will carry a sign

signifying nothing but my own
third eye imprinted with Om,

the universe at a standstill.
Yoga for all times, I say,

for the Raj again, or the Mughals
in-between – oh, and the Aryans,

Emperor Akbar himself – what
the *Vedas* compel us to accept

in each new generation. Now, being
at the ghats in Rishikesh, or some place

like it north or south of the border –
holier than before – what I must

contemplate, or will always cherish
as I keep longing for nirvana – is freedom

across India, despite Partition,
with belief only in eternity.

Making compelling gestures,
reciting mantras from days gone by

at my ashram retreat, meeting
a maharishi eye to eye – more than

the Beatles ever did – I long for
this drumming – reincarnation

in my own spiritual style, declaring
my own tryst with destiny.

THE NICEST BOY

He came to me in the midst of pain,
patted my hand, my forehead,
and cooed soft words

as the bus lumbered on
along the Delhi Road to Agra.
I was still determined

to see the Taj Mahal, to learn
about Emperor Shah Jahan's
love – such devotion.

Again he hummed soft words
and patted my hand, his style,
with his mother looking on,

she who had worked in Siberia
as an engineer, she said,
without a husband.

The boy kept smiling about what
his mother knew from long ago
about her son's winning ways,

and I closed my eyes, imagining
The Taj Mahal and Mughal walls
coming down, a miracle I conjured,

and the boy kept smiling, making
history with me, it seemed, as his
mother looked on all the while.

PART FOUR

HINTERLAND

Consider the forest – roots, stones, rocks –
where I want to be with you
in its farthest reaches, with a clamorous heart
thinking of the jaguar, whispering amongst ruins,
vines, tangles of undergrowth, where the beast snarls,
and a heavy tongue whips out at daybreak –
memory of former days and nights,
as we come to grips with worlds coming closer

in the hinterland of giant fish, arapaima,
and birds like the horn-bill in moonlight,
stars moving of their own accord to the mouth of a cave,
or to where mangrove and courida beckon,
the ocean coming closer. What I want to welcome
among ruins, again in a coral reef…
my palpitating breath in an ark of survival

dreaming of former days and nights, places
I never wanted to be, and palavering with words,
a heave and a sigh, shape or memory, I hear –
a story told in one breath, in one place only, in time.

OWL NIGHT

1.
In hallowed time, it flew in,
and I shut the door tightly.

Such a night I remember
in the house built on stilts.

Now, being away too long
memory's gone awry,

and when I come back
looking for this one bird,

a real owl, believe me,
I inhale deeply.

2.
Trade winds blow across
cane-fields, coming much

too close. I wanted to
distance myself from it,

see in pitch blackness,
but the bird's shrouded

as I didn't want it to be.
Now in half-light

I claim it, over the years,
mythical as Asia.

3
I searched on tables, chairs,
going under the bed, looking

in every corner for an owl's
eyes, for a genuine bird

making night-sounds,
a hoot from not far away,

but it kept itself mysterious,
a behemoth silhouetted

against the moon; though,
being a bird most of all,

from the beginning
bursting out in dreams.

Shadows everywhere,
I breathe harder because

of what's passing through,
what's undone, gone away.

HAWK

i

Hawk came down in a slant of sun
mirrored against galvanized zinc,
somersaulting along the horizon
as a lone lamb frisked.

Hawk was now ready to dive,
taking aim in the sun's glare,
eyes locked to the ground,
to the one object only.

Lamb sensed the commotion
of beating feather, of shadow,
wings flapping. Darkness,
quivering mightily.

Wool sizzled, flesh pulsed
and began to crack like dried clay,
the brain in heat blazing out
like a volcano.

ii

Hawk buffeted, plummeting down,
then quickly heaved up
with a chunk of flesh,
pulling hard, defying gravity.

Defying man's watchful eye,
it rose higher, with the sheep's
bleating like a thousand bells
in meadows everywhere

Hawk soared in unison with
the wind like a song,
going higher, thinking of
when it would break morsels

of flesh from wool and feed
its young, for life to continue
in a nest, blood flowing through
a heart without frenzy or regret.

BIRDING THE CAGE

1
Narrow corners and crevices,
sheer apparatus or design,
the poem's form of rhyme,
rhythm – all in one fell
swoop. Bird-swoop,
imagery moving about
at will in the cage,
wings aflutter.

Making something
out of nothing, a voice
with its own utterance,
whether sublime, or an epiphany
the spirit can conceive of,
though heavy-laden with words,
the shape of things to come,
ascendant in mid-air.

2
Transcendence I long for,
like a bird's egg
that keeps being renewed
in the cage, with bars, doors
everywhere, but nowhere a hand seen…

Escaping to an orchard
I keep coming closer to leaves,
going back in time to roots,
to more words and their origins.
Birdsong, you see,
this craft I bear: a beginning
and an ending, a making and
unmaking   once again.

HISTORY'S MOMENT

Under an umbrella sky,
standing on
this soggy face

of earth,
I look at a worm
on the asphalt

slowly crossing
with a mind of
its own, it seems,

as I contemplate
what's in-between
or what's behind,

lighting up the dark
moment I now
contend with.

History's path's
a heartbeat away;
the worm's own

I'm left to behold
standing upright,
listening only.

Plop-plop-plop
rain coming
down hard

JAWALLA

Where the Mazaruni
and Kukui rivers meet
in the Amazon
sits Jawalla.

This Amerindian village
where gold mines, casak
and religion come together,
is no Eden.

The Mazaruni River
is polluted now
and everywhere's
the same.

Night-time comes too soon,
without serenity
when the generators
take over.

It's no longer silent
as the villagers
grapple with it,
taking in the bad

with the good,
they say. Yes,
the village is
moving on.

Sitting on the banks
of the Mazaruni,
Jawalla is silent.
I know

the Akawaio word
for "Big Jaguar"
I now hear,
AAAAGGH!

JAGUAR

The jaguar pretends
to be a jaguar, just

make-believe, though with
paws, eyes, ears, teeth —

yes, teeth indeed —
when suddenly it snarls

and the forest heaves;
a loud roar next,

the sound going round
and round in my head,

as I follow the beast
to its lair at the edge of

the forest where there's
a cave — Plato's no doubt.

Imagining the beast's head,
its eyes emblazoning

like diamond beads, the jaws
opening wider, teeth jutting out,

I want to withdraw,
as my heart pounds,

but it's too late when
the jaw-door suddenly snaps

shut, and I close my eyes,
thinking nothing's left,

a void being all

WILSON HARRIS: LAND SURVEYOR

All the world's epics from genesis on
are here, where greenheart is at the centre,
with measurement, compass, gauging
and theodolite too. By a benab
in camp he looks up at the forest canopy
with a Blakean eye, where wallaba and mora
trees grow taller. With instinct of spirit,
he ponders the anaconda below
as the eagle soars in the empyrean sun;
in dream or fantasy, moving
over rapids in a corial in darkening time,
his spirit-level reads the middle ground
of rivers, tributaries... a tapestry of stars,
the peacock's eye now luminescent.
Old Schomburgh coughs because
of what's always in men's minds –
Death-in-life from Sorrow Hill,
a dreamer's maze, labyrinthine from early,
as Christ's tiger again flicks
its tail at raindrops in this ritual
up the Essequibo to the Pomeroon.
Now the whole armour of God's
in Demerara, Abary and Berbice
as he keeps watch for hidden tacouba,
circumspect for time's foreboding,
surveying terrain where cliffs rise higher,
the imagination being all;
                          the Carib bone-flute's
his objective correlative at Mariella
in this Amazon's gothic House of Usher;
or it's an El Dorado of lost time,
the Arawaks' own place long before
Sir Walter Raleigh came to take its maidenhead;
but it's in New Amsterdam where Harris lived

his early years in Guyana, his words
like tortoise shells, carapaces hiding
provenance of sun and stars, revealing
what Frank Boaz or Claude Levi-Strauss
never thought about. With his compass
he flitted back and forth in circular
time, one with Homer's Odysseus
and Telemachus, charting the spirit's course,
               Donne in his dream-boat
moving against the river's tide, palace
of the peacock becoming archetype
in the cliff-face not far ahead. Seen
from a gorge, what he reflected upon
in his poetry was eternity to season…
the forest's rhythm in more unheard
voices, the water-level rising and
new pathways seen from aerial
photographs – all maps of the mind,
or the mask of an old Arawak woman's
face formed by unnameable gods;
rain coming down hard, thunder and lightning
too, back to the sea of the savannah
with more rapids and waterfalls.
In his constant eye and reverie,
Wapishana and Wai-Wai images,
a boa-constrictor shedding its skin,
or the pork-knockers' desire to find
legendary El Dorado: all this he
reflected upon, making him prescient
from the start, coming to grips with
Carroll's music being everywhere,
Wishrop and Vigilance in Mariella,
the moon and the sun, garimpeiros
from Brazil and Venezuela.
               Looking up at the ibis
and macaw transcendental in the azure

sky, the forest's hubris, traversing
coastal waters again in Potaro, Bartica,
Cuyuni, Mazaruni and Tumatumari;
making the far journey of Oudin, with Ram
forging an unknown destiny, with Beti
vulnerable in indentured time;
with Magda and Sharon too, he looked
to elusive Cristo with a carnival body,
while Blake's tyger burned brighter
                    — nebula of a dark star —
mythic in his tropes, figurations;
in the Canje journeying with Fenwick
in the boat's gunwale, then Donne or black
Poseidon with slave memory in Baracara —
more dreams coming alive in the timeless
ascending of the secret ladder…
As the snake sheds elemental skin —
the shape-shifter and bone-spirit
with vestiges of pentecostal longing
in each leaf and bark of tree —
the more Harris gauged the water,
his spirit-level rising, by Dutch
Kyk-over-Al's plantation fort,
the chalk-bone of history, while
the eagle keeps looking down on
spectral men in the boat's bow,
close to where a lone capybara grazes
amongst water-hyacinth, the dream-boat
steering closer to a portage, the dead
coming alive again, longer days and nights
ahead, as a phantom jaguar sniffs the ground,
rosettes of its coat falling like stars
in the spider-web of dreams, sublime
music heard as Carroll whistles long
and hard — echoes being all.

THE PEACOCK'S EYE

— found poem

The dark notes
rose everywhere,
so sombre they broke
into a fountain of light,
a rainbow sparkling
from invisible sources;
as the savannah grew lonely
when the sea broke again
into a wave,
through the forest
tall trees carried black
marching boots with
feet clad in spurs; and
sharp wings of a butterfly
flew and vanished
into the sky, making
a sound so terrible
and wonderful
it was sorrowful
and mystical too,
speaking with the inner
longing of a woman,
or the deep mystery
of a man — frail, nervous,
and yet grounded;
as I listened,
what I understood
was that no living ear
on earth can
truly understand
the fortunes of love,
or the art of victory

over death without
mixing blind joy
with sadness…
the sense of being
lost with the hope
of being found,
once again.

ABOUT THE AUTHOR

Cyril Dabydeen was born in the Canje, Guyana. His father was a marginal cattle farmer, his mother a seamstress. He grew up with his grandmother and an extended family of aunt, nieces, nephews. His grandfather, a driver on the Rose Hall sugar estate, died when Cyril was very young, and the family survived through running a small-scale cakeshop.

When he left school, he worked as a pupil teacher at the St Patrick's Anglican School. He began writing in the 1960s, winning the Sandbach Parker Gold Medal for poetry in 1964; his first collection of poems, *Poems in Recession*, was published in 1972.

In the early 1970s he left Guyana for Canada to obtain higher education, and he obtained a BA at Lakehead University, an MA and an MPA at Queens University. From the late 1970s he wrote and published energetically, establishing his reputation as an important new writer in Canada and the Caribbean. He has published four novels, seven collections of short stories and fifteen collections of poetry and edited several important collections of Canadian-Caribbean writing.

He has been a literary juror for Canada's Governor's General Award for Literature; the Neustadt International Prize for Literature and the James Lignon Prize Competition (the American Poets University & College Poetry Prize Program) and the Bocas Litfest (Trinidad).

He has been a finalist four times for Canada's Archibald Lampman Poetry Prize, as well as for the Guyana Prize. He received the City of Ottawa's first award for Writing and Publishing, and a Certificate of Merit, Government of Canada (1988) for his contribution to the arts. He is a regular book critic for *World Literature Today*.

He worked for many years in human rights and race relations in Canada, and taught in the Dept. of English, University of Ottawa.

OTHER CYRIL DABYDEEN TITLES

The Wizard Swami
ISBN: 9780948833199; pp. 136; pub. 1988; price: £7.99

A richly observed comedy that deals with the fate of Hindu ideals in secular and cosmopolitan Guyana as a rural Hindu teacher finds multi-racial Georgetown a confusing place and discovers the dangers to religion's truths when they serve ethnic assertion.

Dark Swirl
ISBN: 9780948833205; pp. 112; pub. 1986; price: £7.99

When a European naturalist arrives in a remote rural village, folk belief confronts rationalistic science in this poetic novel which explores the Guyanese legend of the monstrous Massacouraman.

Berbice Crossing
ISBN: 9780948833694; pp. 148; pub. 1996; price: £8.99

Short stories spanning the crossing between the Caribbean and North America, set variously in the urban melting pot of Toronto and the unsettling landscapes of rural Berbice with its ferocious crocodiles and even a spliff-toting Rasta.

Discussing Columbus
ISBN: 9780948833571; pp. 96; pub. 1997; price: £7.99

This collection of poems explores experiences of Canada and the Caribbean which simultaneously speak of a past of brutal genocide and a world of recreating newness, constantly evolving from the convergencies which that voyage of 1492 began.

Imaginary Origins
ISBN: 9781900715942; pp. 254; pub. 2004; price: £9.99

From more than thirty years of published work, and drawing on eleven individual collections, Cyril Dabydeen selects those poems that best represent the imaginative journey he has made across multiple boundaries – India, Guyana and Canada – and the rich heterogeneity of his vision.